THE NUREMBERG TRIALS

The Investigation into Crimes Against Humanity

Written by Quentin Convard
In collaboration with Antoine Baudry
Translated by Jessica Foster

History | 50MINUTES.com

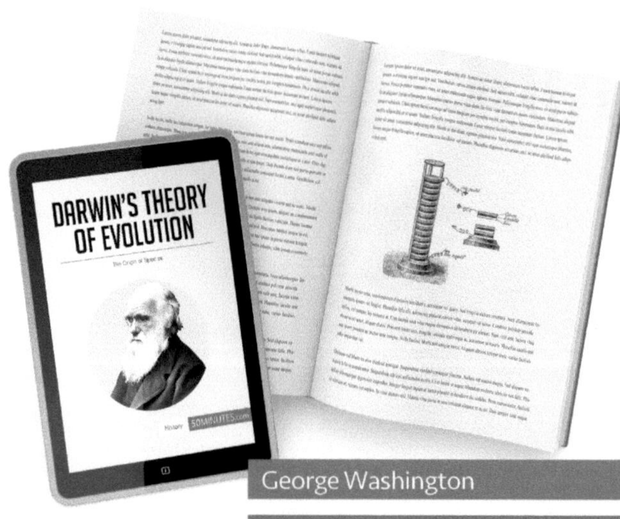

50MINUTES.com

BECOME AN EXPERT
IN HISTORY

George Washington

The Battle of Austerlitz

Neil Armstrong

The Six-Day War

The Fall of Constantinople

www.50minutes.com

THE NUREMBERG TRIALS

KEY INFORMATION

- **When:** 20 November 1945-1 October 1946.
- **Where:** Nuremberg (Germany).
- **Context:** end of the Second World War.
- **Key protagonists:**
  - Lord Justice Geoffrey Lawrence, British judge (1880-1971)
  - Robert H. Jackson, US Supreme Court Justice (1892-1954)
  - Hermann Göring, marshal of the Third Reich (1893-1946)
  - Albert Speer, Minister of Armaments of the Third Reich (1905-1981).
- **Impact:**
  - The establishment of the International Criminal Court.
  - The development of legal definitions of the concepts of crimes against peace and humanity, and of genocide.

INTRODUCTION

While the Second World War was still ongoing, the nations who were victims of the horrific actions of Adolf Hitler (1889-1945) wanted the crimes that had been committed to be recognised and ruled on. For the first time in history, an international military tribunal took place. The trials, which took place in Nuremberg, Germany, took legal action against 24 Nazi leaders and eight organisations, all accused of conspiracies, crimes against peace, war crimes and crimes against humanity. Between 20 November 1945 and 1 October 1946, 401 hearings, during which 94 witnesses were questioned and thousands of pieces of written evidence analysed, uncovered the truth about the Nazis' deplorable actions. This allowed the four appointed judges, representing the Allied countries (United Kingdom, United States, France and the Soviet Union), to reach an unbiased verdict.

But the Nuremberg trials were also part of a broader context, that of international criminal jurisdiction. This was its first real application and as such led to new reflections on how to give rulings following a war, paving the way for the establishment of other international courts. The verdicts also provided a precedent for the legal definition of the concepts of crimes against peace, crimes against humanity and genocide. The media coverage of the debates and the hopes of those who had been oppressed by Nazi Germany made these trials a major turning point in the legal history of the 20th century.

CONTEXT

HOW CAN WE RULE ON WAR?

From the second half of the 19th century onwards, weaponry had advanced at an astounding rate and the professional standing army was gradually integrating with the conscript army, making the distinction between soldier and civilian increasingly difficult. In order to better regulate war and limit crimes, international law tried to draft legislation using treaties that came to shape the criminal history of the time. The Paris Declaration Respecting Maritime Law of 1856 and the First Geneva Convention of 1864, "for the Amelioration of the Condition of the Wounded in Armies in the Field", were drafted in this context. Two fundamental texts were used in conjunction with these two treaties: the Hague Conventions of 1899 and 1907, which defined the laws and customs of war on land, emphasising disarmament and conflict prevention.

However, the First World War (1914-1918) and the use of toxic gases, the deportation of civilian populations and submarine warfare blew all these regulations out of the water. Although no trial was held at the end of the conflict, there was still a certain amount of reflection to determine the responsibilities of each country. The Treaty of Versailles of 1919 pointed the finger at Wilhelm II (German Emperor and King of Prussia, 1859-1941), who was considered to be responsible for initiating the hostilities, due to the violation of Belgium and Luxembourg's neutrality. The British Prime Minister David Lloyd George (1863-1945) went as far as demanding that the German monarch be hanged. An extradition request was also made by the Netherlands so that they could bring the emperor to trial themselves. In addition, one article of the Treaty of Versailles required the German government to hand the individuals accused of war crimes over to the Allied powers. But the Netherlands refused, and this demand of the Treaty of Versailles was not met. However, the *Reichsgericht* ('Imperial Court of Justice'), the highest judicial authority in the German Empire, received the authorisation to try war criminals. Thus began the Leipzig War Trials, which were held in the *Reichsgericht* from 1921 to 1922. Only one of the 16 prosecutions led to a conviction, that of Ludwig Dithmar, who was found guilty of torpedoing a Canadian hospital ship and was sentenced to four years in prison. However, compared with the horrors committed during the war, these rulings were seen as entirely farcical by the Allied countries.

CONVICTIONS OF CRIMES IN THE SECOND WORLD WAR

During the interwar period, various treaties were ratified on the subject, in many of which the idea of punishing not only the States, but also natural persons acting within these States, can be found. The Nuremberg trials constituted the first attempt at an international response to the crimes committed by the main Nazi leaders during the Second World War.

Throughout the war, the leaders of the Allied powers defended the idea that those responsible for the fighting should be tried at the end of the conflict. From 17 April 1940 onwards, the French, English and Polish governments publicly condemned the atrocities committed towards the Jews in Poland. One year later, the American president Franklin D. Roosevelt (1882-1945) also denounced the immoral crimes committed by Nazi leaders, an accusation that was supported by the British Prime Minister Winston Churchill (1874-1965), who also wanted the Nazi's deplorable actions to be punished.

In line with this idea, the Declaration of St James's Palace, which set out the basis for international jurisdiction, was ratified by representatives from incumbent governments and governments from occupied countries who were in exile in London on 13 January 1942. General Charles de Gaulle (1890-1970), upon signing this text, asserted his desire to punish the guilty parties and to not make the mistakes of the Treaty of Versailles again.

On 30 October 1943, the Moscow Declarations, signed by the United Kingdom, the United States and the Soviet Union, established the jurisdiction under which those who had committed war crimes would be tried: if the offenses had been committed in one country, they would be tried there; if on the other hand the acts took place in multiple territories, they would be convicted following a joint decision on the part of the Allies. It said nothing, however, about how to proceed if there was a difference of opinion. During the Tehran Conference (1943), Franklin D. Roosevelt and Winston Churchill stated that they wanted the defendants to be executed without a trial, but Joseph Stalin (Soviet head of state, 1878-1953) rejected this suggestion. When President Harry S. Truman (1884-1972) came to power, the American position moved towards the idea of an international trial, of which de Gaulle seemed to be in favour. The concept gained ground and, following Armistice, was accepted by all parties.

PREPARING THE TRIAL

Harry S. Truman immediately tasked the Supreme Court Justice Robert Jackson with preparing the trial. Jackson went to London on 20 June 1945 to discuss his organisation with his British counterparts. The Americans wanted to centre the hearings on the accusation of a Nazi conspiracy and crimes against peace, in order to convict those who had declared, prepared and organised the war. They also wanted to bring the organisations that had helped the Nazi system to function to trial, but they did not yet know if one long trial would be enough. The British, on the other hand, wanted the sentencing to be done quickly above anything. The two countries found a middle ground and the British judges put forward the first names of those to be tried.

On 24 and 25 June, French and Soviet delegations also arrived in London. As their countries had been the main location of the offenses, they rejected the central idea of crimes against peace, preferring the concept of war crimes. In fact, in their opinion, it was not the act of having declared war that posed a problem, but rather the means used throughout the conflict. After lengthy negotiations, the four nations managed to reach a compromise. On

8 August 1945 the four-party London Charter, which set out the regulations and procedures for the trials, was signed, and the International Military Tribunal of Nuremberg was established. The Allied countries represented all the other states that had accepted the London agreements. Thus France represented Belgium, Luxembourg, the Netherlands and Norway, for example.

The charges were also finalised in the agreement drafted in London. There were originally three of them: crimes against peace, war crimes and crimes against humanity – the latter aimed particularly at punishing the organisation of the deportation and systematic massacre of unarmed civilians. However, these three types of crimes did not cover all of the Nazis' wrongdoings, and some defendants thus risked slipping under the wire. Consequently a fourth charge was added – and in fact became central – namely, the idea of participation in a conspiracy.

The idea of 'conspiracy' came from English law and was a foreign concept to French and Soviet jurists. The Americans and Brits therefore had to lobby extensively to allow this charge to appear in the trials. This notion comes from the idea that an infraction, having been premeditated and thought up by several people in secret, constitutes a crime.

THE LIST OF DEFENDANTS

The definitive list of defendants was not drawn up overnight. The British and American delegations first settled on ten people who had had significant responsibilities in the Nazi regime. The British delegation added seven more, including

Adolf Hitler, who had not yet been officially declared dead. However, his name was removed on 18 October 1945, the day the trials began, when the four countries agreed on the final list. In total, 24 Nazi leaders were to be tried:

- Hermann Göring, *Reichsmarschall* (1893-1946)
- Rudolf Hess, Deputy Führer and Head of the Nazi Party Chancellery (1894-1987)
- Joachim von Ribbentrop, Minister of Foreign Affairs of the Third Reich (1893-1946)
- Robert Ley, head of the German Labour Front (1890-1945)
- Wilhelm Keitel, chief of the *Oberkommando der Wehrmacht* (1882-1946)
- Julius Streicher, publisher of the anti-Semitic newspaper *Der Stürmer* (1885-1946)
- Ernst Kaltenbrunner, SS general (1903-1946)
- Alfred Rosenberg, Nazi racial ideology theorist and Leader of the Foreign Policy Office of the National Socialist Party (1893-1946)
- Hans Frank, Governor-General in Poland in 1939 (1900-1946)
- Wilhelm Frick, Minister of the Interior of the Third Reich (1877-1946)
- Hjalmar Schacht, Economics Minister of the Third Reich (1877-1970)
- Arthur Seyss-Inquart, *Reichskommissar* for the Netherlands and SS *Gruppenführer* (1892-1946)
- Karl Dönitz, German admiral named by Hitler as his successor (1891-1980)
- Walther Funk, Economics Minister of the Third Reich after Schacht (1890-1960)

- Albert Speer, Minister of Armaments and War Production of the Third Reich (1905-1980)
- Baldur von Schirach, head of the Hitler Youth (1907-1974)
- Fritz Sauckel, Nazi leader who was notably responsible for deporting labourers from occupied countries (1894-1946)
- Alfred Jodl, chief of the German *Wehrmacht*'s Operations Division (1890-1946)
- Franz von Papen, Hitler's Vice-Chancellor (1879-1969)
- Konstantin von Neurath, SS general (1873-1956)
- Erich Raeder, Commander in Chief of the *Kriegsmarine* (1876-1960)
- Martin Bormann, SS general and advisor to Hitler (1900-1945)
- Hans Fritzsche, head of the news division of the Nazi Propaganda Ministry (1900-1953)
- Gustav Krupp von Bohlen und Halbach, German industrialist (1870-1950).

But when the trial began, three of these men were not present at the court: Gustav Krupp was declared unable to be tried due to the state of his health, Martin Bormann was nowhere to be found – he had almost certainly died following the Battle of Berlin in May 1945 – while Robert Ley had been found hanged in his cell one month earlier.

As well as these natural persons, for the first time, Nazi regime organisations would also be tried. Following the discovery of the extermination camps, eight organisations were targeted: the Nazi Government, the National Socialist German Workers' Party (NSDAP), the SS (*Schutzstaffel*, 'Protection Squadron'), the Gestapo (*Geheime Staatspolizei*,

'Secret State Police'), the SD (*Sicherheitsdienst*, 'Security Service'), the SA (*Sturmabteilung*, the paramilitary wing), the German General Staff and the High Command of the German armed forces.

After defining the charges and the list of indicted individuals and organisations, the Allied countries had to find a place that was suitable for hosting the trials, the defendants, the various delegations and the many journalists who wished to report on this unique event. The city of Nuremberg, then under American occupation, was chosen for two reasons:

- The first reason was a symbolic one. This city, where the NSDAP held meetings every year, was the ideological capital of the Third Reich.
- The second was more practical. At the end of the war, Germany lay largely in ruins, but the city of Nuremberg, despite having been bombed by Allied forces in 1945, had managed to keep some of its buildings intact, including the infrastructure necessary for the organisation and smooth running of the trials. The Palace of Justice was in fact still usable and was unusual in that it was directly linked to the prison by an underground tunnel, which strengthened security.

KEY PROTAGONISTS

LORD JUSTICE GEOFFREY LAWRENCE, BRITISH JUDGE

Geoffrey Lawrence during the Nuremberg trials.

Originally from Builth Wells in Wales, Geoffrey Lawrence was born on 2 December 1880 to a British noble family. He studied at Haileybury and Imperial Service College, where he befriended Clement Attlee (1883-1967), the future Prime Minister, before being accepted to New College, Oxford.

Once he had finished his studies, he joined a barrister's

chambers that specialised in taking appeals to the English high courts, until the First World War broke out. During the war he joined the Royal Regiment of Artillery and was even appointed to the Distinguished Service Order. At the end of the war, Lawrence pursued his career as a legal practitioner and specialised in cases of appeal before the King's Counsel, the consultative body that advised the monarch on British legal affairs. In 1927 he entered the King's Counsel and became the Attorney General to Prince Edward of York (1894-1972) until 1944, when he was made a Lord Justice of Appeal.

On account of his extensive legal experience, he was chosen by his peers as the head of the British delegation at the Nuremberg trials and was later made President of the judges at the trial. His counterparts chose him in order to pay homage to the courage shown by Great Britain during the conflict. Once the trial was over, he was raised to the peerage, meaning that he was a judge in the House of Lords, and joined the Judicial Committee of the Privy Council, where he would remain until his retirement in 1957. He received the title of Baron Oaksey in 1947 and inherited the title of the Baron of Trevethin around ten years later. When he retired, he moved to his home in Wiltshire to dedicate himself to his passion, horse breeding, and died on 28 August 1971 at the age of 91.

ROBERT H. JACKSON, SUPREME COURT JUSTICE

Picture of Robert H. Jackson.

Born on 13 February 1892 in Pennsylvania, Robert Jackson grew up in the state of New York and set his heart on a legal career very early on. At the age of 18, he joined a law office as an apprentice in Jamestown (New York). He founded his own practice in the same town after graduating from Albany Law School and presided there for around twenty years. Jackson was close to President Franklin D. Roosevelt and was appointed by him to federal office in 1934. He occupied different positions there until 1940, when he was made United States Solicitor General. A year later, he became a Supreme Court Justice, a position he held until his death.

Jackson was gifted with an impressive way with words and eloquence, and in 1943 wrote up the Barnette judgement, a text stipulating that children were no longer obliged to say the Pledge of Allegiance in schools. A year later, he was again involved in a historic judgement in the *Korematsu vs. United States* case, which contested the legality of the imprisonment of Americans of Japanese origin on the West coast during the Second World War.

Given his outstanding career as a jurist, he was chosen by President Harry S. Truman to prepare the Nuremberg trials and became a chief prosecutor. At the end of the trials, Jackson continued his career as a Supreme Court justice and died on 9 October 1954 at the age of 62.

HERMANN GÖRING, *REICHSMARSCHALL*

Hermann Göring pictured in his cell in Nuremberg.

Hermann Göring was born in 1893 and sent to a cadet school in Karlsruhe in 1908. While the first few years of his education had been fairly mediocre, the former layabout left this institution with excellent grades and was accepted into a military academy in Berlin. He left there in 1911 with the status of non-commissioned officer, ready to follow the same military career as his father.

During the First World War, he distinguished himself in the air force, which led to him being awarded the *Pour le mérite* medal in 1918. While his beginnings were promising, a scandalous speech in which he blamed the German government led to his exclusion from top responsibilities. He then became an airline pilot for various commercial companies and campaigned as part of several small nationalist groups. He met Adolf Hitler in 1922 and they got on well, and he became one of his closest collaborators when he was named commander of the SA.

Following the failed Beer Hall Putsch in Munich on 8 November 1923, Göring was shot twice in the leg. While he was being treated for his injuries, he developed a taste for morphine and soon became addicted. He then left Germany for Austria due to an arrest warrant against him and stayed in his wife's homeland, Sweden, for four years. During this exile, his mental state deteriorated, as did his health.

Once an amnesty had been declared, he returned to Germany, where he was elected a representative of Bavaria in 1928. This was the groundwork for a fast-growing political career. In 1932, following the landslide victory of the National Socialist Party, Göring was chosen as the President of the Reichstag (legislative chamber). In 1933, he became the Commissioner of Aviation before being put in charge of the economics plan for war in 1936. He played a major role in the persecution of Jews and the implementation of concentration camps.

When war broke out, Göring was met with a great deal of sympathy in German public opinion. However, as commander of the *Luftwaffe* (German air force) and a close advisor to Hitler, he had a record of failure and bravado, which greatly annoyed his chief, who nonetheless refrained from criticising him in public. The aviator ended up being disgraced and was a victim of the schemes that shaped life in the Third Reich. His sworn enemies, including Martin Bormann, defeated him: he was placed under house arrest at the end of the war and sentenced to death by the Führer, who nonetheless thanked him for his services. He gave himself up to the Americans and joined the other defendants at the Nuremberg trials. Found guilty on all counts, he was sentenced to death in 1946.

ALBERT SPEER, MINISTER OF ARMAMENTS AND WAR PRODUCTION OF THE THIRD REICH

Albert Speer pictured in his cell in Nuremberg.

Born in 1905 to a well-off family, the young and athletic Albert Speer followed the same career path as his father and grandfather, who were both architects. Following his graduation, he became the assistant of the renowned architect Heinrich Tessenow (1876-1950), and married Margarete Weber (1905-1987) in 1927. Although he was not particularly interested in politics, he was struck by the character of Adolf Hitler during a protest and joined the Nazi Party in 1931. After carrying out various tasks within the organisation, he was chosen by Joseph Paul Goebbels (1897-1945) to renovate the party's headquarters in Berlin. When Hitler became Chancellor in 1933, Speer was again called upon by Goebbels to renovate the Ministry of Public Enlightenment and Propaganda.

In the same year, he met the Führer for the first time during the preparation for the Nuremberg Rally, the general convention of the National Socialist Party. Subsequently, the Chancellor regularly took interest in the young architect's work and made him part of his inner circle in 1934, rapidly promoting him to the head of the Chief Office for Construction. In the 1930s he was put in charge of several impressively large projects, notably the Party's rally grounds, where the Nuremberg Rally was held every year, and the German Pavilion for the international exposition in Paris in 1937. He also helped with the construction of the Olympic stadium in Berlin. However, his main project was the new Reich Chancellery, which had been bombed and destroyed by Allied forces at the end of the war. He also created an immense plan for rebuilding Berlin. During these years, Speer nurtured a solid friendship with Hitler, which led him to confirm, during the Nuremberg trials, that "if Hitler had any friends at all, [he] certainly would have been one of his close friends" (Fest, 1999).

In 1942, following the death of Fritz Todt (1891-1942), Speer became Minister of Armaments and War Production, a position that he accepted hesitantly and which made Göring jealous. On top of his ministerial prerogatives, he had to contend with Goebbels, Bormann and Minister of the Interior Heinrich Himmler (1900-1945), who all dreamed of taking his place. When the Reich was in decline, Speer kept his distance from Hitler, and disobeyed him by refusing to carry out his scorched earth policy in occupied areas of Germany. After seeking refuge in Hamburg, he was arrested by the Americans on 15 May and cooperated with them.

After the Nuremberg trials, Speer carried out his prison sentence in the Spandau prison until October 1966. He then spent the end of his life writing books about the Third Reich, which make up some of the richest witness accounts on the period. He died in 1981 at the age of 76.

THE NUREMBERG TRIALS

THE OPENING OF THE TRIALS

Photo of a tribunal session in Nuremberg.

While the inaugural session took place in Berlin on 18 October 1945, the true beginning of the trials was on 20 November 1945 in Nuremberg, and was marked by the reading of the indictment by the prosecutors from each Allied nation, which lasted almost five hours.

The defendants. First row, from left to right: Hermann Göring, Rudolf Hess, Joachim von Ribbentop, Wilhelm Keitel. Second row, from left to right: Karl Dönitz, Erich Raeder, Baldur von Schirach and Fritz Sauckel.

The following day, the defendants had to state whether they were pleading guilty or not guilty. All of them chose the second option. Hermann Göring, one of the most senior dignitaries of the Third Reich, was the first to be questioned. While he tried to make a statement, he was soon called to order by President Lawrence, asserting his authority from the outset. Jackson, a chief prosecutor, then read the opening statement in which, using a selection of clever and well-constructed arguments, he revealed the prosecution's viewpoint and explained the reason he was on trial by anticipating the criticisms that could be made of it.

DID YOU KNOW?

Every speech was translated simultaneously, a great novelty at the time, which meant that the speakers had to speak slowly. In order to make the translation as perfect as possible, there were several bright warning lights in front of the speakers, controlled by the translators, which lit up if the speaker had to repeat their sentence or slow down.

THE HEARINGS' PROCEEDINGS

At the court's request, the prosecution and the defence then presented their evidence and called up their witnesses. All the evidence was essentially written documents, mostly from the official archives of the Third Reich, and had been discovered by the Americans. In total, 5000 documents and 7000 works of Nazi literature were analysed. One of the key sources in the trials was the diary of Hans Frank (1900-1946), the Nazis' Governor-General, nicknamed the "butcher of Poland" following his role in exterminating Jews in the country. Written evidence was extremely important as it was enough to sentence the defendants.

94 witnesses took the stand in 10 months, not only to corroborate the written facts, but also to give the trials a universal impact and make Nazi crimes more personal. Witnesses for the prosecution, then for the defence, were questioned in turn, and the judges could speak at any time to ask a question. Only the intervention of Friedrich Paulus

(German marshal, 1890-1957), on 11 February 1946, brought new information to the long deliberations. The former soldier came to be a witness for the Soviets on the subject of the extermination of Russian prisoners by German troops, causing Göring and some of the other defendants to jump to their feet and shout in the courtroom, claiming that Paulus's position was hypocritical. Paulus had already been a critic of Nazism during the war and was respectful of the Geneva Convention, and had become an instrument of Soviet propaganda following his capture by the Russians during the Battle of Stalingrad (1942-1943). The defendants subsequently considered him to be a traitor who had defected to the enemy side.

While the prosecution only called a few concentration camp victims to the stand, the defence did not hesitate to take advantage of a large number of witness accounts. This led to some powerful scenes, such as when Rudolf Dies (1900-1957), leader of the Gestapo between 1933 and 1934 and Göring's protégé, was called to the stand to defend Göring with regards to the incident of the Night of the Long Knives.

THE NIGHT OF THE LONG KNIVES

Between 29 June and 2 July 1934, Hitler executed the leaders of the *Sturmabteilung* (SA) of Ernst Röhm (1887-1934), nicknamed the Brownshirts. They had terrorised Germany since 1926 and contributed to Hitler's rise to power, and had recently been perceived as an organisation with too much importance. The main purge took place on the night between 29 and 30 June

1934, and allowed the Chancellor to rally conservative groups and the army around his cause. The general population had no choice but to accept the event.

As the International Military Tribunal mostly followed English and American law, the defendants were allowed to be witnesses at their own trials. As such, after four months of deliberation, Göring was the first to take the stand. This was one of the pivotal moments of the event. While answering his lawyer's questions, Göring charmed the audience and made fun of the prosecutor Robert Jackson, who struggled to hide his annoyance, much to the audience's amusement. After a forced weight loss regime and cured of his morphine addiction, the *Reichsmarschall* spoke like a man who knew he was damned and did nothing to hide his actions. He managed to charm the public, win the duel against the American prosecutor and strengthen the courage of the other defendants. He ended his deposition with a six-hour diatribe in which he reasserted his belief in Nazi ideology.

Göring at the trial.

Another noteworthy deposition was that of Albert Speer. An architect of the Third Reich as well as the Minister of Armaments and War Production, he surprised the audience by admitting responsibility for his involvement, whereas the others, emboldened by Göring's intervention, opted for an arrogant line of defence without questioning the Nazi regime or Hitler's actions. The architect who, at the time of the events, had tried to improve conditions for workers under forced labour and stood up to Hitler regarding the end of the war by refusing to implement the scorched earth policy, gained the clemency of the court with his self-criticism.

A FLOOD OF REVELATIONS

Through the chief prosecutors, the Nuremberg trials managed to shed light on the deportation of populations, economic looting, crimes, the war at sea and the genocide of the Jews. The manipulative madness of the Nazi leaders, as well as the plot carried out to legitimise the attack on Poland, was revealed to the whole world.

OPERATION HIMMLER

In order to legitimise the attack on Poland, Hitler decided, along with the leader of the Gestapo Heinrich Müller (1900-1945), and following the plan devised by his trusted colleague, Himmler, to give around a dozen German prisoners lethal injections. They were then riddled with bullets, disguised as Polish soldiers and laid around the Gliwice radio station, in an image aiming to make the whole world believe that the Polish had been the first to attack the Germans on 31 August 1939. Known under the name of 'Operation Himmler', this plot enabled the Führer to justify the deployment of his troops to Poland on 1 September 1939.

One of the key issues in the Nuremberg trials was the genocide of the Jews. The prosecution, made up of various prosecutors from the Allied nations, called several witnesses to the stand to explain the process of exterminating the Jewish population. The director of the Auschwitz-Birkenau camp, Rudolf Höss (1900-1947), the former leader of *Einsatzgruppe*

D (the armed political police of the Third Reich), Otto Ohlendorf (1907-1951), and the former SS member, Dieter Wisliceny (1912-1948), took the stand and told the judges about the methods used by the Nazis to eradicate populations. A documentary showing the discovery of the extermination camps by the Allies was also shown, leading to varying reactions among the defendants. While Hans Frank burst into tears, Göring tried to defend himself by evoking the *Führerstaat*, the idea that the state is ruled by a leader who is the only one responsible, as everyone else must obey him blindly. But the French deputy prosecutor, Edgar Faure (1908-1988), shattered Göring's defence.

SOVIET GREY AREAS

Certain events described during the trials caused unease for the Soviets. While the USSR had paid a great price during the conflict, their presence at the victors' side was not disputed, but that does not mean that they were exempt from all blame. Indeed, two points mainly cast doubt upon some Soviet actions, which the Nuremberg trials did not manage to fully uncover or solve: the secret pact between the Germans and the Soviets and the Katyn massacre.

On the first point, nobody was unaware of the pact of non-aggression between Hitler's Germany and the USSR, signed in 1939. But the trials revealed another secret agreement between the two nations, which anticipated a sharing of territories between the two signatories once the conflict and the annexation were over. The Soviet prosecutor, Roman Rudenko (1907-1981), tried to prevent this information from being revealed by all means possible so that it did not become public knowledge, but the tribunal believed it important to know the truth about this matter, however unflattering it was for the Soviets. Although the agreement had now been discovered, the USSR was still not under legal investigation.

Mentioned in the indictment, the Katyn massacre was an even thornier issue, one which would not end up appearing in the final judgement. The central question, debated during the trials, was about the date on which the atrocities against the Polish people had been perpetrated. While the Germans insisted that the massacre had been committed in the spring of 1940 by Soviet troops, the second Soviet prosecutor, Pokrovsky, stated that the events had happened in the autumn of 1941, when Katyn Forest was under German rule. Both the defence and the prosecution presented three witnesses who incessantly contradicted each other. After two days of heated debates, the tribunal was unable to discern the lies from the truth.

THE KATYN MASSACRE

The atrocity committed by the Soviet political police, the NKVD, in the spring of 1940 is emblematic of the crimes committed by the USSR during that period against the Polish population. On Stalin's orders, Polish prisoners, who were against Communist ideology, were killed by a bullet to the back of the neck. 11 000 deaths were counted between August 1941 and the spring of 1943. While Stalin tried to blame these executions on the Nazis, a report by the American Congress in the 1950s established the Soviets' responsibility for the massacre. Subsequently, on 14 December 1992, the Russian president Boris Yeltsin (1931-2007) sent his Polish counterpart, Lech Walesa (born in 1943), a copy of the documents signed by Stalin that proved the killing.

DELIBERATIONS

On 31 August 1946, after nine months of the trial, the defendants had the opportunity to make a final statement which would be re-broadcast on the radio before the announcement of the verdict, set to take place on 1 October. In order for the verdict to be delivered, the judges had to deliberate. While all of them could give their opinions, only the specifically appointed judges had the right to vote on the punishments and, for a decision to be made, the majority of these judges had to agree. In the event of a tie, it fell to President Lawrence to decide. While the idea seemed simple, the deliberation over the fate of some of the defendants gave rise to long discussions. This was, for example, the case for Rudolf Hess, Hitler's Deputy Führer and an official representative of the Nazi party. While the English and American judges wanted to sentence him to life imprisonment, the French judge wanted to give him 20 years, whereas the Soviet judge voted for the death penalty. He would eventually receive a life sentence. The case of the economist Hjalmar Schacht also led to long discussions. Lawrence was in favour of acquittal while the Soviet judge wanted the death penalty. On the French side, five years' imprisonment was requested, while the United States asked for life imprisonment. Ultimately, the economist would be acquitted.

Another problem arose during the deliberations regarding the execution of the defendants. The judges had to determine how those sentenced to death would be executed, and opinions also differed on this matter. The Soviet Union was in favour of execution by firing squad, instead of the humiliating death by hanging desired by Lawrence and the United States judge. France suggested deciding on a case by case basis. Although the other judges in the proceedings backed this suggestion, all those who were sentenced to death would be hanged.

THE VERDICT

The day before the verdict was announced, 30 September 1946, the chief prosecutor Jackson read his judgement and presented his final requisitions. The crimes of the Nazi regime and of the defendants were thus reviewed. On the morning of 1 October, Lawrence, President of the Tribunal, took the floor and the individual decisions were given one after another. To the surprise of the audience, three of the defendants were acquitted. They were the journalist Hans Fritzsche, the diplomat Franz von Papen and the Economics Minister Hjalmar Schacht. The first, a close friend of Joseph Goebbels, was recognised as being anti-Semitic but never contributed to the extermination or even the persecution of the Jewish people. The second, ambassador to Turkey during the war and the third, imprisoned in Dachau following the failed attack on the Führer in 1944, were judged to be cowards, but could not be found guilty by the court of the crimes committed by the other defendants.

After the lunchbreak, the session continued and the 19 men found guilty came in turn into the dock to hear their sentences: 12 death sentences and seven prison sentences. Of the 24 defendants, we must also note that Martin Bormann, believed to have fled, was sentenced to death *in absentia*, Gustav Krupp was extremely unwell and had been declared unfit to stand trial and Robert Ley had committed suicide before the trial. The reactions to the sentences varied depending on the defendant, and some of them filed petitions for mercy for various reasons. Alfred Jodl, Chief of the Operations Staff of the Third Reich's armed forces, and Wilhelm Keitel, chief of the Supreme Command of the German armed forces, demanded their right to be executed by firing squad. Erich Raeder, Commander-in-Chief of the *Reichsmarine*, asked if he could be sentenced to death instead of suffering a life imprisonment sentence. Göring's lawyer, on the other hand, tried to change his client's death sentence into a life imprisonment sentence, without Göring asking him to. The guilty parties had four days to appeal, but none were accepted. On 15 and 16 October 1946, those who had been sentenced to death were executed by hanging, apart from Göring who committed suicide by swallowing a cyanide capsule the night before.

As for the organisations, four of them were sentenced and declared criminal: the NSDAP, the SS, the SD and the

Gestapo. The idea that the members of these associations would be sentenced at the same time was abandoned due to concerns over time. The judges would then have to try to determine whether or not they were aware of the objectives of the organisations to which they were affiliated and whether or not their joining was voluntary. While the SA and the *Reichsregierung* did not receive a collective sentence, this did not prevent members of these groups from being sentenced subsequently during denazification trials.

DENAZIFICATION

At the end of the war, the Allies began a legal and legislative process aiming to get German society back on the track of democracy and to punish the Nazis who had committed crimes during the war. The denazification trials were presided over by the Germans, with the support of Allied powers. Almost 5000 Nazis were sentenced, but often for minor wrongdoings. The evidence was difficult to collect and the Germans were above all worried about their own survival.

THE FATE OF THOSE WHO WERE ACQUITTED OR IMPRISONED

The three men who were acquitted did not walk free, however, and had to appear in a denazification court in West Germany. Thus, Franz von Papen was sentenced to eight years of forced labour. He was released following an appeal in 1949 and he tried unsuccessfully to make a late return to politics, then spent his final years writing many works in which he tried to explain himself. Hjalmar Schacht was also sentenced to the same punishment, but was freed in 1950. He founded a bank and acted as an advisor to political groups until his death in 1970. Hans Fritzsche was serving a sentence of nine years of forced labour when he was also released in 1950 due to the state of his health. He died three years later.

Those who were found guilty at the Nuremberg trials were taken to Spandau Prison (West Berlin) nine months later, under the control of the 'Four Powers', and had different fates:

- Konstantin von Neurath, Walter Funk and Erich Raeder were released for health reasons in the 1950s, and all died a short while later.
- Karl Dönitz, Grand Admiral of Nazi Germany, was released in 1956 after serving his ten-year sentence. Two years later he published his memoirs, and he died in 1980 from a heart attack.
- Albert Speer, freed in 1966, wrote several works containing rich sources of information on the people and structure of the Third Reich. He died in 1981.
- Baldur von Schirach, head of the Hitler Youth, was also freed in 1966. He was unwell and retired to south-west Germany, where he died in 1974.
- Rudolf Hess died in prison in 1987 at the age of 93. He hung himself in his cell, but his suicide was contested by his family who believed that he had been assassinated.

This theory was also supported by neo-Nazi groups, who saw him as a martyr. For many years after his death, extremist groups organised an annual march in his memory in the town of Wunsiedel.

Covered globally by the media, the Nuremberg trials faced several opinions criticising their legitimacy. The Soviets and the French communists were outraged by the acquittal of three of the Nazi dignitaries, while the English and American Conservative parties criticised the harshness of the verdicts. But the ideological complaints were the strongest. The Four Powers were reproached for organising the trials because they wanted to avenge themselves, and the fact that no Germans attended the hearings went down very badly. The German historian Rudolf von Thadden (1932-2015) insisted notably on the fact that some Germans resisted Hitler and also found themselves imprisoned in concentration camps. However, their voices had not been heard.

IMPACT

INTERNATIONAL JURISDICTION

Many trials aimed at punishing Nazi crimes followed those at Nuremberg. One, in particular, was a direct result of it. It was that of Adolf Eichmann (1906-1962), a high-ranking official of the Third Reich who was captured by Israeli agents in Argentina and sentenced by the young Hebrew state in April 1961. Due to its extensive media coverage and the definition of its charges, the trial undoubtedly resembled the Nuremberg trials. Moreover, Eichmann's part in the 'Final Solution' (Jewish genocide) had been discovered during the hearings presided over by Lawrence. The objective of the trial was to give the extermination of the Jews a human dimension, to allow the spectators to identify with the deported populations, which Nuremberg did not manage to do. The defendant was eventually sentenced to death by hanging and was executed on 31 May 1962.

The Nuremberg trials and Eichmann's trial became real sources of inspiration for similar trials in the years that followed. On 25 May 1993, the UN Security Council thus created an international court in The Hague in order to judge the crimes committed in former Yugoslavia. This was a step towards creating permanent jurisdiction, following the example of the court in Arusha (Tanzania), tasked with giving a ruling on the atrocities carried out in Rwanda in 1994. After being petitioned for decades, the International Criminal Court was set up at the end of the 1990s. However, although its statute was signed on 17 July 1998, the creation of the Court officially dates from 1 July 2002.

DEFINING CRIMES AGAINST HUMANITY

The concept of crimes against humanity appeared for the first time during the Nuremberg trials and belonged in a precise context. Following Article 7 of the Rome Statute of the International Criminal Court (1998), it took on a broader sense and is defined as follows: "[s]erious crimes committed against civilian populations as part of a widespread and systematic attack. The Statute of the International Criminal Court lists the serious crimes as: murder, extermination, enslavement, deportation or forcible transfer, unlawful deprivation of liberty, torture, rape and other serious sexual violence, collective persecution, enforced disappearances, apartheid and other similar inhumane acts causing great suffering or serious injury" (*Oxford Dictionary of Law Enforcement*). It is worth noting that, during the Nuremberg trials, the genocide of the Jews was not legally considered a crime against humanity, as the link between a war of aggression and persecution of this religious group had not been established. As evidence that this concept evolved in the second half of the 20th century, Klaus Barbie (German police officer, 1913-1991), nicknamed the "Butcher of Lyon", appeared before the Assize Court of the Rhone in 1987 on the count of crimes against humanity due to his responsibility in the deportation of Jews from France.

SUMMARY

1945
8ᵗʰ May: **Germany surrender**
20ᵗʰ June: Robert H. Jackson is tasked with preparing the Nuremberg trials
18ᵗʰ Aug.: Inaugural session of the trial in Berlin
20ᵗʰ Nov.: **Official beginning of the trials**

1946
13ᵗʰ May: Göring takes the stand
Sept.: Deliberations
30ᵗʰ Sept.-1ˢᵗ Oct.: The verdict is given

2002
17ᵗʰ July: **Creation of the International Criminal Court**

The Nuremberg Trials © 50MINUTES.com

- While the Second World War was still raging, the Allies expressed the idea that Nazi Germany should be punished for the atrocities it committed. Leaving the war victorious, the Allies set up the International Military Tribunal in order to judge the leaders of the Third Reich.
- On 20 June 1945, the Supreme Court Justice Robert H. Jackson was entrusted by the American President Harry

S. Truman with travelling to Europe and organising the trial, which would take place in Nuremberg, a former pillar of the Nazi regime, with the Allied nations (Great Britain, the USSR and France).

- The final list of defendants was established on 18 August 1945, the day of the inaugural session of the trial in Berlin. It contained the names of the 24 high-ranking Nazi officials and the eight organisations of the Third Reich. Among them, three defendants were not present during the trials: Martin Bormann was thought to be on the run, Gustav Krupp had been declared medically unfit and Robert Ley had killed himself in his cell a short time earlier.

- The trials officially began on 20 November 1945 in Nuremberg with the reading of the charges: conspiracies, crimes against peace, war crimes and crimes against humanity. All the defendants pleaded not guilty.

- For several months, the prosecution and the defence presented their evidence in turn and called their respective witnesses to the stand to corroborate the evidence. In total, 94 witnesses were heard from in the space of ten months.

- On 13 May 1946, the defence had the floor, and Göring was the first to take the stand. For eight days he charmed the audience and openly mocked Jackson, the chief prosecutor, while reaffirming his adherence to Nationalist Socialist ideology. The other notable intervention was that of Albert Speer. Unlike Göring, the official architect of the Third Reich criticised himself, thus gaining the clemency of the jury.

- The Nuremberg trials revealed a large amount of information concerning Nazi conspiracies to exterminate populations. Some grey areas regarding Soviet actions were also pointed out. Although the role played by the Soviet Union in the Katyn massacre remained unclear, the secret pact they signed with Hitler's Germany, which detailed how annexed regions would be distributed, was revealed.

- In September 1946, the judges began to deliberate. The verdict was given on 30 September and 1 October. Of the 24 defendants, 12 were sentenced to death, including Martin Bormann *in absentia*, seven were sentenced to imprisonment and three were acquitted. Additionally, four of the eight prosecuted organisations were declared criminal (the NSDAP, the SS, the SD and the Gestapo).
- The Nuremberg trials received much criticism, but they were the first example of international jurisdiction and would lead to the creation of the International Criminal Court. The verdict would also create a legal definition of the concepts of crimes against peace and crimes against humanity.

We want to hear from you!
Leave a comment on your online library
and share your favourite books on social media!

FURTHER READING

BIBLIOGRAPHY

- Casamayor, L. (1985) *Nuremberg: 1945, la guerre en procès*. Paris: Stock.
- De Fontette, F. (1996) *Le procès de Nuremberg*. Paris: PUF.
- Delpa, F. (2006) *Nuremberg : Face à l'histoire*. Paris: L'Archipel.
- Fest, J. (1999) *Speer: The Final Verdict*. Boston: Harcourt.
- Garapon, A. (2002) *Des crimes qu'on peut ni punir, ni pardonner*. Paris: Odile Jacob.
- Gilbert, G. (1947) *Le journal de Nuremberg*. Paris: Flammarion.
- Goldensohn, L. (2005) *Les entretiens de Nuremberg*. Paris: Flammarion.
- Gooch, G. and Williams, M. (2015) *Oxford Dictionary of Law Enforcement (2nd edition)*. Oxford: Oxford University Press.
- Merle, M. (1949) *Le procès de Nuremberg et le châtiment des criminels de guerre*. Paris: A. Pedone.
- Sereny, G. (1974) *Into That Darkness*. London: Pimlico.
- Varaut, J.-M. (1992) *Le procès de Nuremberg*. Paris: Perrin.
- Wieviorka, A. (2005) *Le procès de Nuremberg*. Caen: Éditions du Mémorial de Caen.

ADDITIONAL SOURCES

- Roland, P. (2012) *The Nuremberg Trials*. London: Arcturus Publishing.
- Sereny, G. (1996) *Albert Speer: His Battle With Truth*.

Santa Cruz: Peter Dimock.

- Taylor, T. (1992) *The Anatomy of the Nuremberg Trials: A Personal Memoir.* New York: Alfred A. Knopf, Inc.

ICONOGRAPHIC SOURCES

- Geoffrey Lawrence during the Nuremberg trials. Royalty-free reproduction picture.
- Picture of Robert H. Jackson. © Harris & Ewing.
- Hermann Göring pictured in his cell in Nuremberg. © United States Army Signal Corps.
- Albert Speer pictured in his cell in Nuremberg. © United States Army Signal Corps.
- Photo of a tribunal session in Nuremberg. © Bundesarchiv.
- The defendants. Royalty-free reproduction picture.
- Göring at the trial. Royalty-free reproduction picture.

50MINUTES.com
History
Business
Coaching
EL DIAGRAMA DE ISHIKAWA
LA GUERRA DE PALESTINA DE 1948
DOMINA EL ARTE DEL NETWORKING
IMPROVE YOUR GENERAL KNOWLEDGE
IN A BLINK OF AN EYE !
www.50minutes.com

© **50MINUTES.com, 2016. All rights reserved.**

www.50minutes.com

Ebook EAN: 9782806289896

Paperback EAN: 9782806289902

Legal Deposit: D/2016/12603/779

Cover: © Primento

Digital conception by Primento, the digital partner of publishers.